Dedication

This book is dedicated to all the reputable high street butchers in the United Kingdom and the people who shop in them every week.

ISBN 978-0-9926915-0-9

First Published 2013

Copyright© JJ Publications Limited
Published by JJ Publications Limited

JJ Publications Limited, Registered Office
44 Leeds Road, Leeds, LS19 6NY

Introduction

Welcome to The Meat Crusade cookbook, a campaign dedicated to saving the high street butcher. In this book you will find beef, pork and lamb recipes that aim to get the most out of your butcher's terrific meat - as well as some interesting side dishes.

The Meat Crusade is run by farmers and meat wholesalers, John Penny & Sons. Our aim is to put the finest butchers' meat back onto British tables by raising awareness in quality and taste and offering a greater understanding of how ethical meat operations work.

Butchers offer not only fantastic meat and service, but a wealth of advice on how best to cook and prepare your meat. With this in mind we've created a range of recipes using a wide variety of cuts of meat and easily sourced ingredients. We do not profess to be highly trained chefs and we have not used a vast array of complicated kitchen gadgets. We think nothing is more off putting to a home cook than a long complicated ingredients list and the need for some new expensive piece of machinery that will only be used once.

Everything we cooked has been thoroughly taste tested by people working on our farm, if they didn't like it then it simply didn't go into the book. We hope that you enjoy cooking these dishes as much as we did and that this book encourages you to go back to your butcher for some great tasting ethically sourced meat.

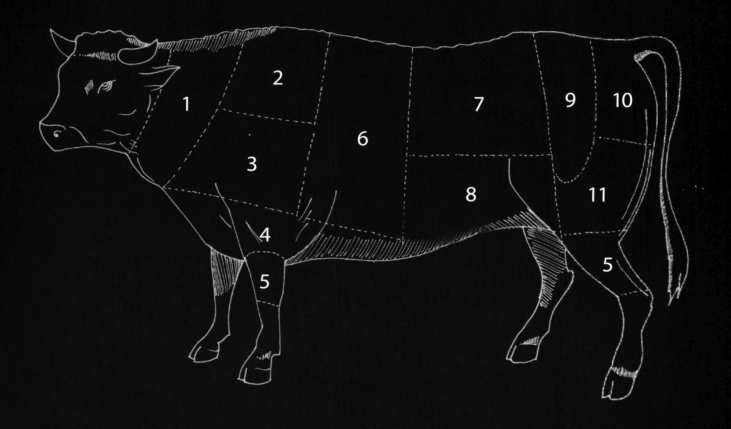

Beef Cuts

1. Neck & Clod
2. Chuck & Blade
3. Thick Rib

4. Brisket
5. Shin
6. Ribs

7. Sirloin
8. Flank
9. Rump

10. Topside Silverside
11. Top Rump

Beef Recipes

The British love of beef goes back for centuries, before the days of singing the national anthem at theatre performances British people would sing "The Roast Beef of Old England" a heart-warming song about how our best national character traits come from eating roast beef.

The pride, care and attention put into raising our beef by responsible farmers is complimented by our lush green countryside which means that as a nation we produce some of the best beef in the world. This is why British butchers are so proud to sell British beef. A reputable butcher will always talk to the farmer who has produced their beef to ensure that the animal has been raised in an ethical, traceable way.

This chapter will not only show you how to cook a traditional roast with Yorkshire puddings but also how you can make your roast go further with handy leftover recipes such as Cottage Pie. We also look at some of the delicious forgotten cuts which you can get from your butcher such as beef shin and Oxtail.

Once you've tried them you'll wonder how they ever went out of fashion.

Beef Bourguignon

Serves 6

Preparation:
15 mins

Cooking Time
2 hours 15 mins
Approx

Beef chuck steak is a great low cost ingredient packed with flavour and this dish shows it off to perfection. Your local butcher will be able to give you top quality chuck steak without any excess fat or additives.

Ingredients

1 kg diced beef chuck steak

1 large carrot, roughly chopped

1 large onion, chopped

2 fresh bay leaves

2 cloves garlic, crushed in their skins

Half a bottle of robust red wine

10 black peppercorns

1 tbsp Port

1 tbsp beef dripping

1 tbsp olive oil

Dijon mustard

1 fresh baguette

How to cook

1. For the best results put the pieces of beef in a large glass bowl and add the next seven ingredients, cover the bowl and leave to marinate in the fridge overnight.

2. Preheat your oven to 140°C / 275°F/ Gas mark 1. Remove the meat from the marinade using a slotted spoon and keep the marinating liquor. In a heavy casserole dish heat the olive oil and dripping until melted then brown the meat off in batches.

3. Using a slotted spoon add the vegetables from the marinade to the pot, and cook for roughly 2 minutes before adding the marinade liquor. The meat should be entirely covered by liquid - if not, add a little more red wine.

4. Move the casserole dish to the oven for 2 hours. Once cooked, remove the pot from the oven and set your grill to the highest setting. Thinly slice the baguette and spread Dijon mustard on one side of each slice.

5. Place the bread slices on top of the casserole dish Dijon side down and place under the grill until golden. Serve with a selection of seasonal vegetables.

Beef Ragu

Serves 4

Preparation:
10 mins

Cooking Time
2 hours 40 mins
Approx

This dish uses chuck which is a great low cost cut of beef which is often used in casseroles and stews. The slow cooking time makes it the perfect weekend supper dish. The whole chilli is optional but adds a touch of heat.

Ingredients

500g diced chuck steak

2 tins chopped tomatoes

1 glass of red wine

1 tbsp Balsamic vinegar

1 tbsp Worcestershire sauce

1 large red chilli, left whole

1 tbsp fresh thyme

300ml milk

3 medium carrots, diced

1 large onion, finely chopped

2 sticks celery, diced

4 large cloves garlic, chopped finely

Salt & pepper

Extra virgin olive oil

Shavings of parmesan

How to cook

1. Heat a small amount of olive oil in a large pan, add the meat in batches and brown and set aside.

2. Reduce the heat and add extra oil to the pan if it's a little dry, now add the onions, celery and carrots and cook until the onions are translucent.

3. Return the meat back to the pan, add the garlic, thyme, chilli (if you want a spicy kick to your dish) and wine. Let the mixture boil for a few minutes to cook off the alcohol, and then add tinned tomatoes. Stir the pan and let it return to the boil. Boil for about 5-10 minutes and then reduce to a simmer.

4. Add Balsamic vinegar, Worcestershire sauce and more salt if necessary, mix and taste. Add the milk and then put the lid on to cook for 2 hours. Stir occasionally and check seasoning.

5. After 2 hours the sauce should have reduced and thickened. Leave it on the heat a little longer if it hasn't. At this point you can remove the chilli or finely chop and stir into the sauce for an extra spicy kick.

6. Serve over pasta with shavings of parmesan and freshly ground black pepper.

Steak Pie

Serves 6

Preparation:
10 mins

Cooking Time
2 hours 45 mins
Approx

This is great comfort food that all the family will love. If you want to make it a steak and ale pie just use 500ml of beef stock and 400ml of ale. Otherwise simply follow the below recipe.

Ingredients

900g diced stewing beef

25g flour, seasoned with salt and freshly ground black pepper

100g butter

2 onions, roughly chopped

2 sprigs fresh thyme

1 bay leaf

900ml beef stock

Salt and freshly ground black pepper

1 whole egg, beaten

300g ready-made rolled puff pastry

How to cook

1. In a bowl dip the meat into the seasoned flour, then place a large lidded pan on the hob.

2. Heat half the butter in the pan and add the meat. Sear all over until golden brown.

3. Add the vegetables and herbs, then pour in the stock. Bring to a simmer, then cover with a lid and gently simmer on the stove for 1½ hours.

4. Preheat the oven to 220° C / 425° F / Gas mark 7.

5. Once cooked, season the stew, add the remaining butter and tip into an ovenproof serving dish with approximately a 6in diameter. Brush the edge of the dish with the beaten egg.

6. Roll out the pastry on a lightly floured surface and then place over the dish. Pinch the edges of the dish so that the pastry will stick to it and trim off any remaining pieces of pastry from around the edge. Cut the leftover pastry into leaves and add them to the top, using the beaten egg as a 'glue' for the decoration.

7. Brush the pastry top thoroughly with the remaining beaten egg and place on a baking tray. Bake in the oven for 15-20 minutes until the pastry is golden brown on top.

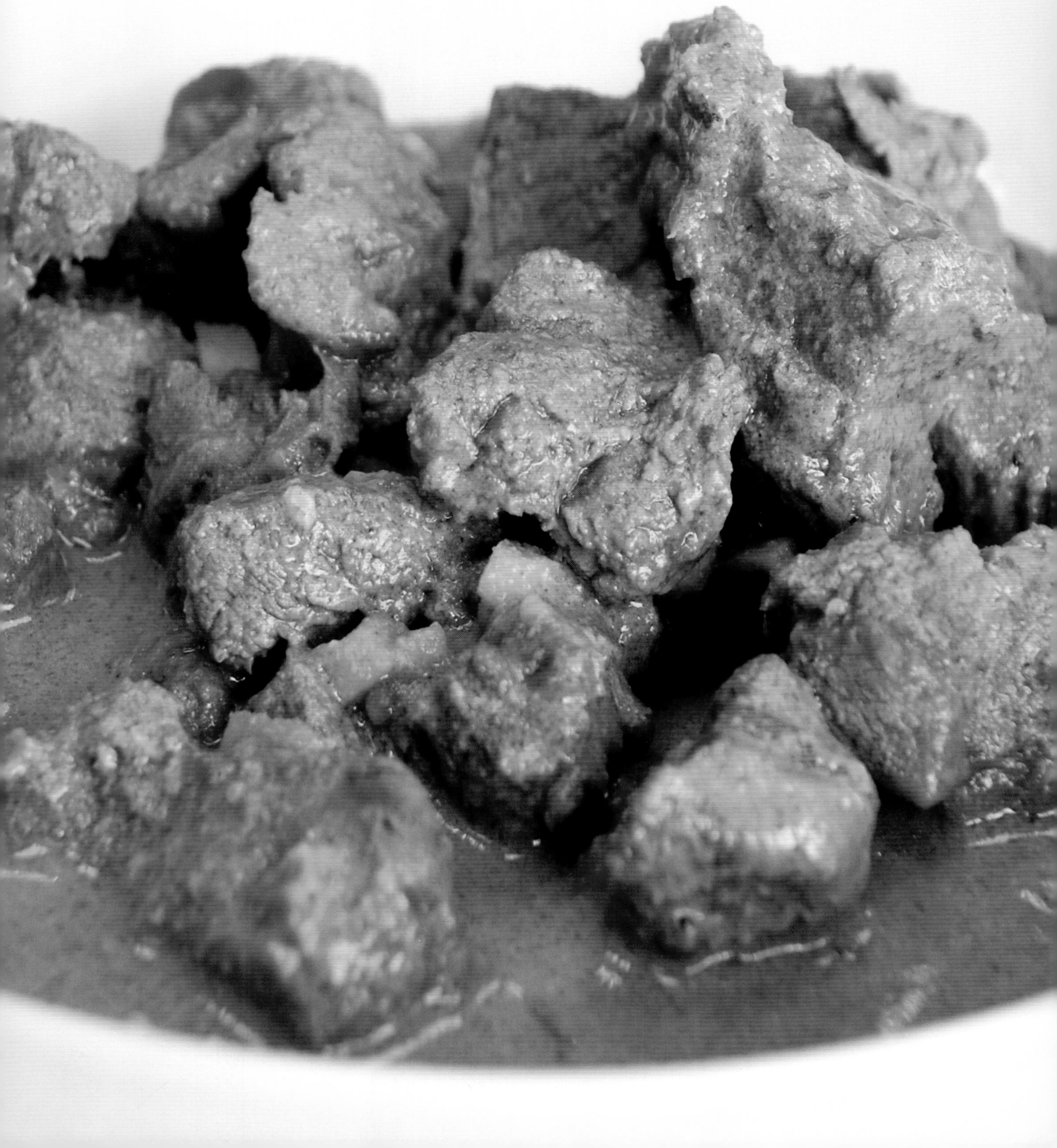

Thai-Style Beef Curry

Serves 6

Preparation:
10 mins

Cooking Time
1 hour 45 mins
Approx

Rump doesn't just have to be served as a steak it is also great in a curry.

Ingredients

Groundnut oil

1 large onion, sliced

1 whole red chilli, finely sliced

2 garlic cloves, crushed

5cm sized piece ginger, peeled and grated

2 tsp turmeric

2 tsp ground coriander

1 tsp cumin

2 tsp paprika

1kg rump steak, cut into cubes

1 can coconut milk

Salt and pepper

How to cook

1. In a large pan heat the oil on a medium heat. Add the onions and cook until translucent, now add garlic, ginger and spices. Cook for a further 5 minutes.

2. Now add the beef and cook until brown. Add the chilli, coconut milk and salt and pepper. Bring to the boil and cover.

3. Reduce heat to a low simmer and cook for 1 ½ hours.

4. Serve with boiled rice.

Smugglers' Shin of Beef

Serves 4

Preparation:
10 mins

Cooking Time
2 hours
Approx

Beef shin is a forgotten cut of meat that works perfectly in slow cooked dishes like this. Your local butcher can easily weigh out the exact amount you need.

Ingredients

900g shin beef, diced

25g flour

25g beef dripping or cooking oil

300ml red wine

450ml beef stock

1 onion, diced

110g cooked beetroot, cubed

Bundle of fresh herbs tied together with string –
bay leaf, thyme and rosemary

Salt and pepper

How to cook

1. Preheat the oven to 150°C / 300°F / Gas mark 2.

2. On the hob, gently heat the dripping in an ovenproof casserole dish until it is completely melted.

3. Now add the beef and fry for 2 to 3 mins, reduce the heat and add the onion. Cook until the meat is lightly browned, stir in the flour and add the beef stock slowly stirring constantly to dissolve the flour and prevent any lumps forming.

4. Add the wine, herb bundle and a pinch of salt and pepper, bring to a rolling boil then pop on the lid. Transfer to the oven and cook for 1½ to 2 hours.

5. Add the beetroot after the first hour.

6. Check the dish regularly and add more wine if it begins to dry out (if it doesn't you can always treat yourself to a cheeky glass).

7. Serve with carrots and new potatoes or any root vegetables you like.

BEEF

Hungarian Goulash

Serves 4

Preparation:
15mins

Cooking Time
2 hours 30 mins
Approx

This slightly spicy dish is a hearty winter warmer and is a great alternative to casseroles.

Ingredients

600g diced beef shoulder

2 tablespoons beef dripping

1 large onion, chopped

2 cloves of garlic, finely sliced

1-2 carrots, diced

400g tin of tomatoes

2 green peppers, thinly sliced

1 tbsp hot paprika

1 teaspoon ground caraway seeds

1 bay leaf

1 pint beef stock

Salt and pepper

1 tbsp soured cream

How to cook

1. In a deep pot heat up the dripping, then add the onions and fry until they are slightly brown. Add the paprika, stirring continuously to prevent burning. Add the beef and cook until brown.

2. Now add the garlic, caraway seeds, tomatoes, carrots, bay leaf and stock, bring to the boil and reduce to a simmer. Season then put on the lid and and cook for 2 hours.

3. Thirty minutes before the end of cooking add the sliced green peppers.

4. Serve with rice or crusty white bread and for extra indulgence add a swirl of soured cream.

Rib of Beef with Horseradish Glaze

Serves 8

Preparation:
10 mins

Cooking Time
1 hour 30 mins
Approx

This classic dish looks stunning when presented on the dinner table for carving, plus it's quick and easy to do! Your butcher can easily French trim this for you.

Ingredients

4.5kg French trimmed rib of beef

2 tbsp of horseradish sauce

2 tbsp of Dijon mustard

2 small cloves garlic, crushed

Vegetable oil

How to cook

1. Preheat oven to 200˚C / 400° F / Gas mark 6. Put the meat into a good sized roasting tin and cook in the oven uncovered for 45minutes.

2. Remove from the oven and mix the horseradish, Dijon mustard and garlic with a little vegetable oil until it is the consistency of double cream. Spread the mixture over the meat.

3. Reduce heat to 180˚C / 350° F / Gas mark 4 and return the meat to the oven. Cook for another 45 minutes. Keep checking the crust so that it doesn't burn. Cover the meat with foil if it looks as though it is burning. These timings will cook the meat to medium, if you prefer your beef well done then cook it for an additional 15/20 minutes.

4. Remove the beef from the oven and cover with baking foil and a tea towel on top, rest the meat for at least 30 minutes before carving to ensure maximum succulence.

5. Serve with your preference of vegetables.

Steak with Pepper Sauce

Serves 2

Preparation: 10 mins

Cooking Time 30 mins Approx

Rump steak is one of the tastiest and cost effective steaks, tell your butcher what you are cooking and they can cut you the perfect thickness.

Ingredients

2 x 175g thick rump steaks

1 tbsp olive oil

55g butter, plus a little more if necessary

2 tbsp Cognac

1 tbsp beef stock

2 breakfast mushrooms

50g Dolcelatte cheese

Sea salt

A pepper mill filled with pink, black and white peppercorns

How to cook

1. Pre-heat the oven to 200°C / 400°F / Gas mark 6. Peel the mushrooms and remove the stalks. Place equal amounts of the cheese in the stalk hole of each mushroom and place on a lined baking tray.

2. Put the mushrooms in the oven for 10-15minutes depending on the size of the mushrooms.

3. Using your pepper mill apply a liberal coating of pepper to both sides of the steaks.

4. Sprinkle a little salt on both sides of the steaks and press the seasoning into the meat.

5. In a large pan heat the olive oil, but don't let it smoke, put the steaks in to cook for 5 minutes then turn and cook for an additional 5 minutes (this will cook them to a medium rare so add a few extra minutes if you like them well done).

6. Add the butter to the pan and allow to foam. Baste the steaks and remove from the pan. Now pour the Cognac and beef stock to the pan and stir well.

7. Pour the sauce over the steaks and serve with the mushrooms and vegetables of your choice.

Beef Stroganoff

Serves 6

Preparation:
10 mins

Cooking Time
30 mins
Approx

This tasty dish is best served with boiled rice. Go to your local butcher who can give you the best sirloin to make this dish.

Ingredients

500g lean sirloin in 2cm cubes

25g salted butter

1 large onion, thinly sliced

1 tbsp plain flour

1 large glass dry white wine

1 tbsp Dijon mustard

250g button mushrooms, halved

How to cook

1. Gently heat half the butter in a large frying pan, add the sliced onion and cook until translucent.

2. Add the meat to the pan and cook until browned all over. Now add the flour and cook for 1 minute before adding half the wine. Reduce the heat and add the mushrooms.

3. Add the rest of the wine and Dijon mustard and simmer gently for 15 - 20 minutes.

4. Serve with wild rice or vegetables.

Fillet of Beef with Pappardelle

Serves 4

Preparation:
15 mins

Cooking Time
40 mins
Approx

Fillet is a bit more expensive than most beef cuts. This hearty dish uses a small amount for a meal that's full of flavour but not too costly on the pocket.

Ingredients

1 white onion, finely chopped

2 celery sticks, finely sliced

1 clove of garlic, sliced

Olive oil

1 tsp chopped fresh thyme

150g beef fillet, cut finely into strips

Table salt

150ml red wine

400g can chopped plum tomatoes

50g butter

1 packet pappardelle pasta

How to cook

1. Cook the onion, celery and garlic in the olive oil in a large pan until softened, and then add the thyme.

2. Increase the heat and fry the beef for five minutes or until softened. Add the wine and tomatoes and simmer over a low heat for 20-25 minutes, or until the sauce is thick and rich.

3. While the sauce is reducing, cook the pappardelle in a large pan of boiling salted water. Drain the pasta and add it to the sauce. Stir in the butter and serve.

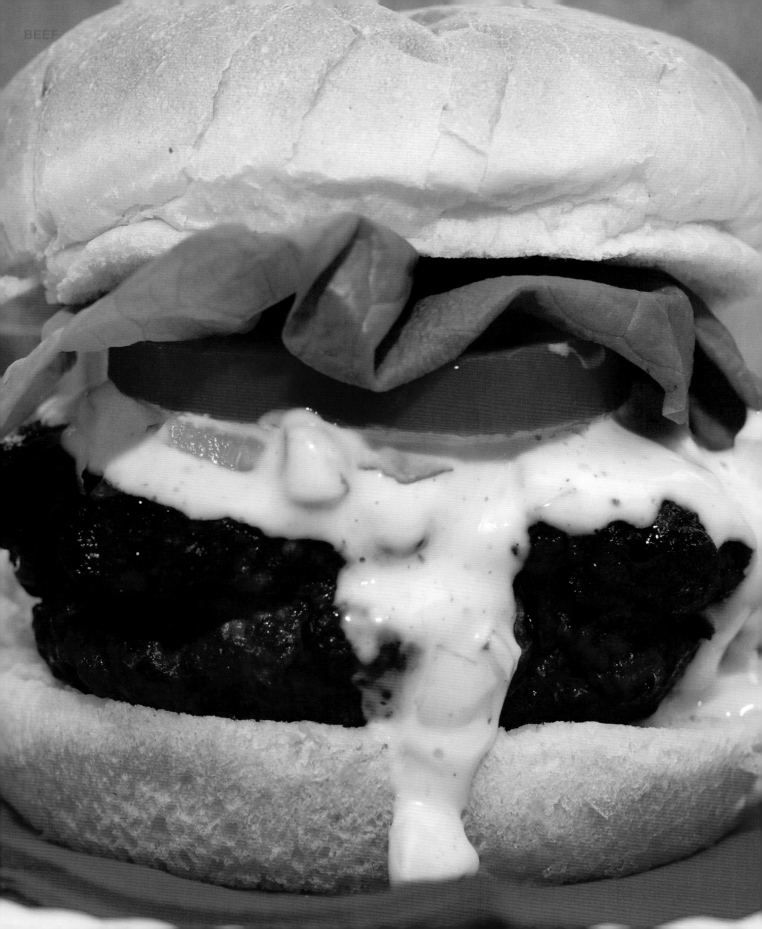

Extra-Juicy Beef Burgers

Serves 8

Preparation: 10mins

Cooking Time 20 mins Approx

The secret to any good burger is the quality of the mince used to make them; your butcher can give you top quality mince with no hidden nasty extras. We've perfected a man sized burger that should satisfy even the hungriest carnivore.

Ingredients

For the burger sauce:

1 tsp Dijon mustard

2 tsp mayonnaise

1 tsp French dressing

1 tsp onion salt

1 tsp garlic salt

2 large gherkins, finely diced

For the burger filling:

1 white onion, finely sliced

50g grated matured cheddar

Vegetable oil

For the burger:

500g minced beef

2 tsp salt

1 tbsp Worcestershire sauce

1 tsp garlic salt

1 egg, beaten

Optional - 8 large burger buns, slices of beef tomato and lettuce leaves

How to cook

1. Combine all the ingredients for the burger sauce in a bowl and mix well, season to taste. Cover the bowl with cling film and leave overnight in the fridge so the flavours can combine.

2. To make the burger filling take the onion and slowly cook in a frying pan with a little oil until golden, then set aside to cool. While the onions are cooling take a large mixing bowl and using your hands combine all of the burger ingredients.

3. Tip the burger mixture out onto a large chopping board and divide into 8 equal portions. Flatten out four of the portions and place equal amounts of the cooked onions and grated cheddar in the centre of each one.

4. Place the remaining four portions on top of the flattened out ones and seal together, ensuring that no cheese or onion is exposed. Place the burgers on a tray and cover with cling film, pop them in the fridge for a minimum of 1 hour (or freeze them to use later if you prefer).

5. Preheat your grill and cook the burgers for a minimum of 5 minutes on either side. If you are barbequing them, still pre-cook for a few minutes under the grill and finish off on the barbeque.

6. Serve in burger buns with the sauce and your preference of fillings, we prefer a few slices of lettuce and some slices of tomato.

BEEF

Beef Lasagne

Serves 6

Preparation:
20mins

Cooking Time
1 hour
Approx

This is a family favourite that can be put together in no time for a flavoursome mid-week supper.

Ingredients

For the meat filling:

1 large onion, peeled and grated

1 large carrot, peeled and diced

2 cloves garlic, finely chopped

1 tsp dried oregano

300g minced beef

1 tbsp tomato puree

1 tbsp Worcestershire sauce

1 bay leaf

1 glass of red wine

1 (400g) tin chopped tomatoes

Olive oil

Sea salt and cracked black pepper

For the cheese sauce:

50g butter

50g plain flour

600ml milk

120g Cheddar cheese, grated

6 dried lasagne sheets

A few drops of tabasco sauce (optional)

Fresh Parmesan, grated

How to cook

1. Preheat oven to 200°C / 400°F / Gas mark 6.

2. Heat the oil in a hot pan and fry the onion, carrot and garlic together. Season with the bay leaf, oregano, Worcestershire sauce and salt and pepper. Cook gently until the onion is translucent. Add the minced beef and cook until browned off.

3. Pour in the wine and cook off the alcohol before adding the tomatoes and puree. Leave to simmer for 20 minutes then turn off the heat and set aside.

4. Melt the butter in a saucepan. Add flour gradually stirring constantly until it forms a paste. Cook gently for 2 minutes then slowly add a small amount of milk, stirring continuously to prevent lumps. Repeat this process until all the milk is used this way may seem time consuming but it is an excellent way of preventing lumps.

5. Season with salt and pepper. Allow sauce to cook for 1 minute before adding the Cheddar cheese and a few shakes of tabasco if you want a bit of a kick. Stir and remove from the heat.

6. Spoon half of the meat sauce into a large baking dish and place lasagne sheets on top. Pour 1/2 the cheese sauce and spread out evenly over the pasta before spooning the remaining meat on top. Add the final layer of pasta and pour the remaining cheese sauce on top.

7. Finish with the grated Parmesan and add a light seasoning of salt and pepper. Place in the oven and bake for 20-25 minutes until golden brown.

Meatloaf

Serves 4

Preparation:
15 mins

Cooking Time
1 hour
Approx

This is a mid-week supper dish that all the family can enjoy. Make sure you buy your mince from your local butcher who can tell you exactly what has gone into it.

Ingredients

1 slice white bread, crusts removed

2 tbsp milk

450g minced beef

1 small onion, finely diced

1 egg, beaten

1 tbsp flour

25g butter

Salt and pepper

How to cook

1. Preheat your oven to 180°C / 350°F / Gas mark 4. Crumble the bread into a bowl, and add the milk and stir with a fork until it is absorbed.

2. Add the beef mince, onion and egg, as well as a little salt and pepper and mix together well. The mixture needs to be moist enough to mould into a loaf but not so wet that it falls apart so keep an eye on the consistency.

3. Place the mixture on a chopping board and mould into a loaf shape with wet hands then dust the loaf all over with flour.

4. Melt the butter in a frying pan large enough to put the loaf in as well as being able to turn it. Ensure the heat is medium and fry the meatloaf gently until it is brown all over.

5. Lift the loaf from the pan and place it into a roasting tin, add about 2 tbsp of cold water and the buttery juices from the frying pan - this makes a delicious gravy as the loaf is cooking.

6. Cover with foil and place into the oven for 45mins and serve hot with vegetables. If you have some leftovers it's great eaten the next day with a fresh salad.

BEEF

Mince Beef and Onion Pie

Serves 2

Preparation:
10 mins

Cooking Time
1 hour 15 mins
Approx

This quick and simple pie is best made with top quality beef mince from your local butcher.

Ingredients

250g minced beef

1 white onion, diced

1 stick of celery, diced

250ml beef stock

1 tsp of plain flour

1 tsp of fresh chopped thyme

1 tbsp of Worcestershire sauce

1 tsp of sunflower oil

1 packet of short crust pastry,
ready rolled

Salt and pepper

1 egg, beaten

How to cook

1. Using a large pan with a lid, heat the oil on a medium heat. Add the onions and celery, reduce the heat to the lowest setting and cover for 10mins.

2. Add minced beef and cook until browned. Stir in the Worcestershire sauce, thyme, flour and cook for 1 minute.

3. Gradually add the beef stock and season with salt and pepper, bring to the boil. Reduce to a gentle simmer, place the lid on the pan and cook for 20 minutes, stirring frequently. Remove from the heat and leave to cool. Meanwhile lightly grease a pie dish, approx 7".

4. Fill the dish with the meat mixture and then place the pastry on top. Cut around the dish to remove the excess pastry then press the edges with a fork to create a crimpled effect. Brush the pastry with a little beaten egg.

5. Cook in preheated oven 170°C / 325° F / Gas mark 3 for 35-45 minutes until golden brown.

BEEF

Bolognese

Serves 4

Preparation:
15 mins

Cooking Time
40 mins
Approx

This family favourite is quick and simple to make, but remember for the tastiest outcome use the best quality mince from your local butcher.

Ingredients

Olive oil

500g minced beef

1 large onion, sliced

2 sticks of celery, chopped

2 carrots, chopped

1 clove of garlic, chopped

1 glass of red wine

300ml of beef stock

1 tin of chopped tomatoes

1 tbsp tomato puree

1 tbsp fresh thyme

1 pack dried spaghetti or tagliatelle

How to cook

1. In a large pan heat the olive oil and onions, celery and carrot on a low heat, pop on the lid and leave everything to sweat for 5 minutes.

2. Add the garlic for 1 minute and stir to avoid burning. Add the minced beef and increase the heat of the hob.

3. Once the mince is browned off add the wine, tinned tomatoes, tomato puree, thyme and beef stock. Leave to simmer for 30 minutes or until the mixture has thickened.

4. While the sauce is simmering cook ¼ of the pasta - or more if you are really hungry.

BEEF

Traditional Roast Beef with Yorkshire puddings

Serves 4

Preparation: 20 mins

Cooking Time 1 hour 20 mins Approx

This is a classic dish that we all know and love. What more do we need to say?

Ingredients

1.5kg beef topside joint

25g beef dripping - ask your butcher for this

English mustard

Freshly ground black pepper

125g plus 1 tbsp plain flour, sifted

1 medium size egg

200ml milk

75ml plus 2 tablespoons water

300ml beef stock

Oil for pattie tin

How to cook

1. Preheat the oven to 200°C / 400°F / Gas mark 6. Place the beef on a rack in a roasting tin. Rub the dripping, mustard and pepper over the joint.

2. Cook the beef for 20 minutes per 500g, plus 20 minutes.

3. Whilst the beef is roasting make the Yorkshire pudding batter. Put 125g of the flour in a bowl, and then add the egg and half the milk. Beat until smooth and add the remaining milk plus 75ml of water.

4. When the meat is cooked, drain off all but 2 large spoonfuls of the meat juices into a small pan. Remove the beef from the oven, cover well with foil and clean tea towels and leave to rest whilst the Yorkshire puddings are cooking.

5. Increase the oven temperature to 220°C / 425°F / Gas mark 7. Heat a 12 section patty tin in the oven, add some oil to each patty, allow to heat for a few minutes and then pour the batter into the hot patty tins. Cook the puddings for 20 minutes or until risen and crisp.

6. To make the gravy, skim the fat off the reserved juices in the pan and bring them to the boil. Blend the flour with the water and stir in. Cook for 2-3 minutes, and then add the beef stock. Simmer gently for a further few minutes and serve with the beef and the Yorkshire puddings.

BEEF

Barbeque Beef Sandwiches

Serves 4

Preparation: 10mins

Cooking Time 40 mins Approx

This is a tasty way to use up leftover roast beef and it makes a great Sunday night supper for the family.

Ingredients

500g leftover roast beef

2 shallots, finely diced

1 tbsp olive oil

5 tbsp barbeque sauce

5 tbsp ketchup

2 tsp Tabasco sauce

2 tsp Worcestershire sauce

450ml beef stock

Salt and pepper

8 white sliced sandwich buns

How to cook

1. In a large, heavy pot, heat olive oil on medium heat. Add the shallots and cook until translucent.

2. Add the beef stock, ketchup, Tabasco, Worcestershire and barbeque sauce, increase the heat to medium and simmer for 30 minutes.

3. Add the beef to the sauce and simmer for 5 minutes. Season to taste with salt and pepper.

4. Serve on the buns with salad of your choice.

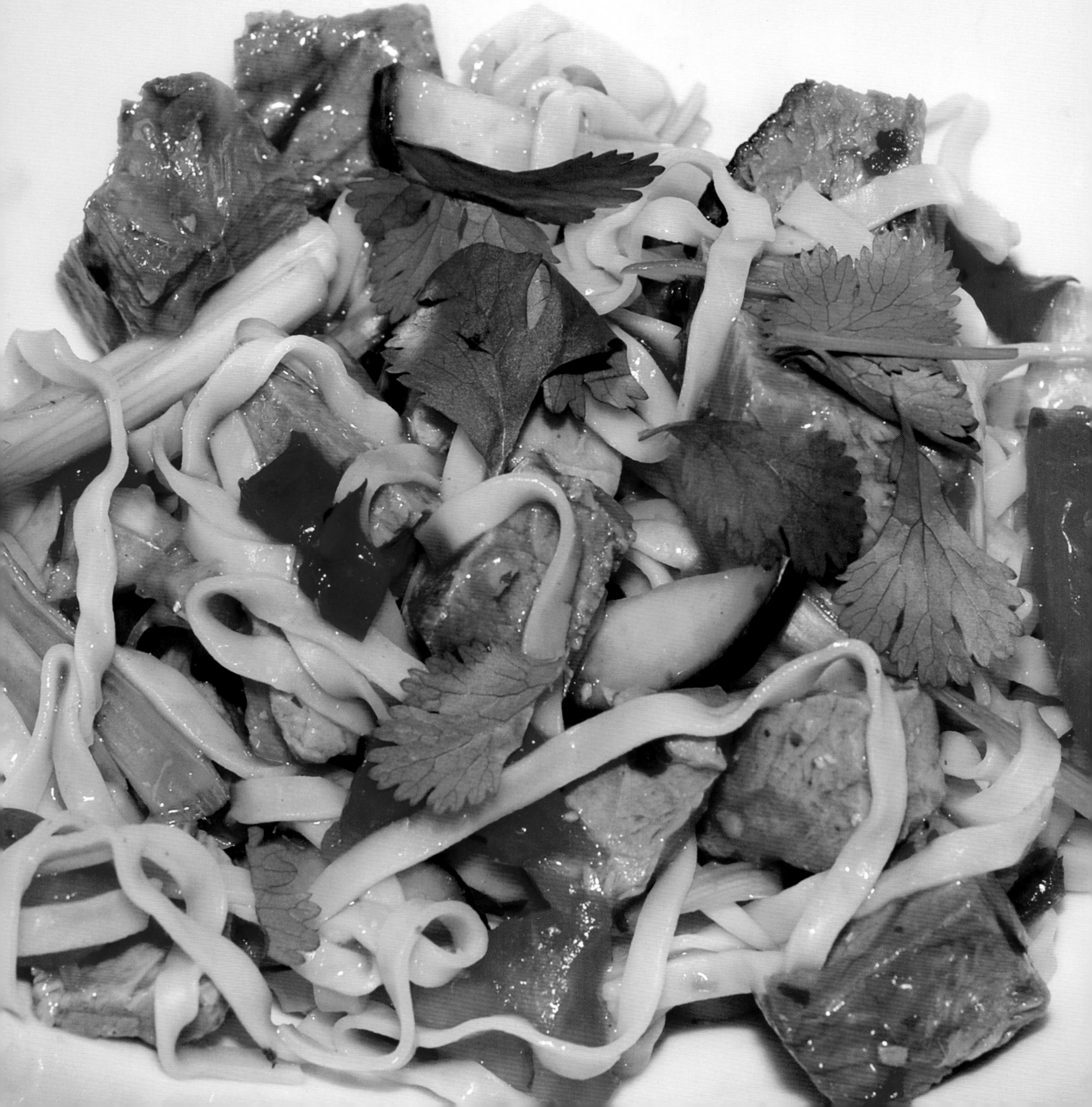

Spicy Beef and Noodle Salad

 Serves 2

 Preparation: 10 mins

This is yet another idea to use up leftover roast beef but in a very different way. Once you've tried it you'll want to make it again and again.

Ingredients

300g of leftover roast beef, cut into bite sized chunks

2 small shallots, thinly sliced

2 plum tomatoes, thinly sliced

2 cloves of garlic, finely minced

1 small bunch of fresh coriander, finely chopped

2 tbsp of Thai sweet chilli sauce

Juice of 1 lime

2 tsp Thai fish sauce

Pinch of salt

1 cucumber, thinly sliced

1 bunch spring onions, thinly sliced lengthways

150g dried egg noodles

How to cook

1. Cook the noodles according to packet instructions.

2. Whisk together the salt, lime juice, chilli sauce, garlic, shallots and fish sauce.

3. Mix the beef, cucumber and spring onion in with the dressing and taste to check the balance of flavours. Add extra chilli sauce or lime as desired.

4. Drain the noodles and add to the beef mixture. Add the coriander and serve.

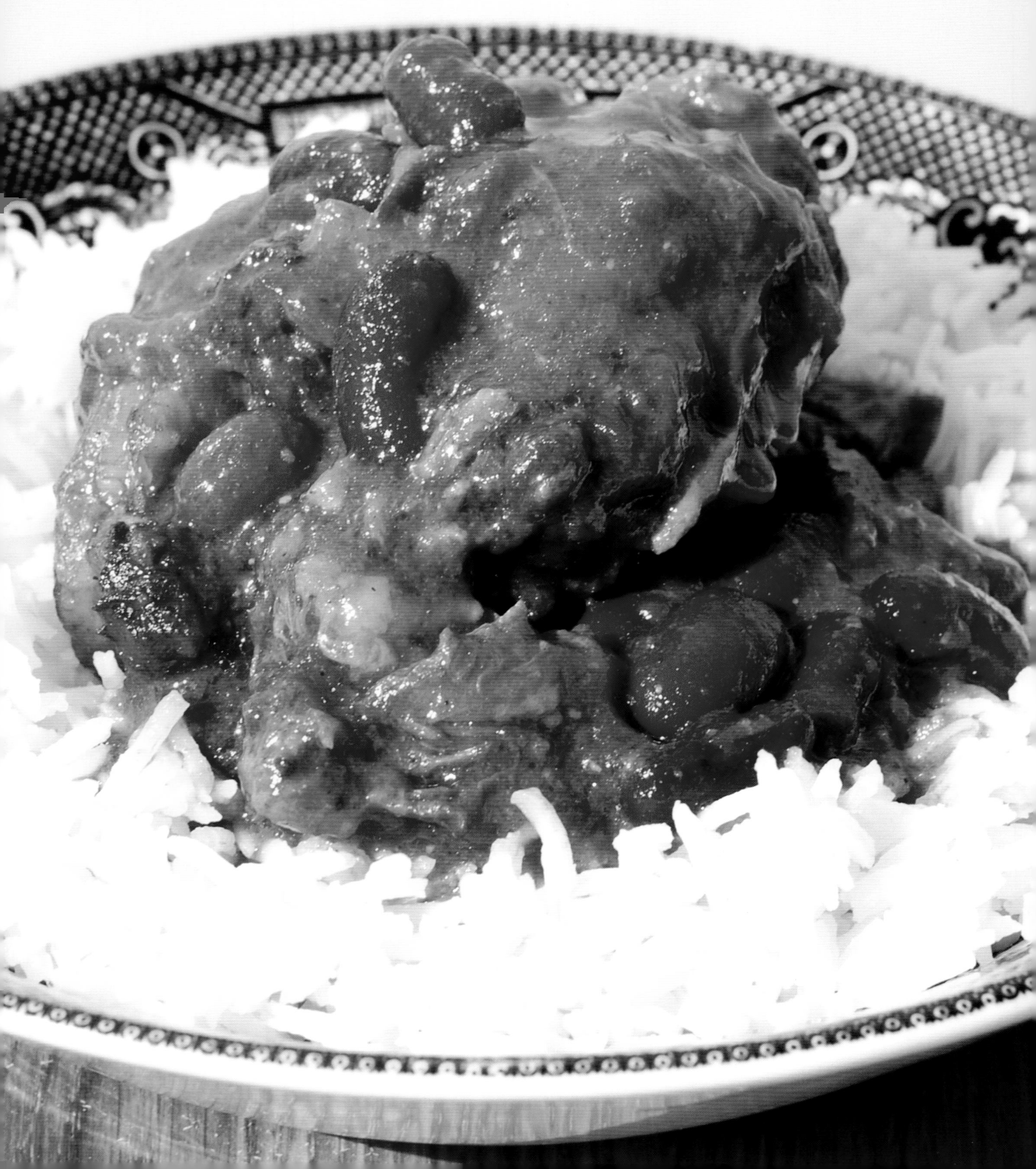

Oxtail Chilli

Serves 4-6

Preparation:
10 mins

Cooking Time
2 ½ hours
Approx

Oxtails are a really tasty cheap cut and this recipe is an exciting alternative to your regular chilli con carne.
By slow cooking this dish the meat falls off the bone beautifully.

Ingredients

3 kilos oxtail, trimmed

200g plain flour, seasoned
with salt and pepper

2 tsp cayenne pepper

2 tsp cinnamon

6 tbsp beef dripping

1 large onion, chopped

4 cloves of garlic, finely sliced

5cm sized piece of ginger,
peeled and finely sliced

2 tbsp Demerara sugar

4 tbsp Dijon mustard

4 tbsp cider vinegar

2 tbsp Worcestershire sauce

1 tbsp lemon juice

1 tsp Tabasco

130g light brown sugar

4 tbsp tomato ketchup

4 tbsp cider vinegar

1 tin chopped tomatoes

1 tin red kidney beans

How to cook

1. Put the flour and dry spices into a plastic bag and mix well. Add the oxtails
   and toss them in the seasoned flour.

2. In a large pan heat the beef dripping. Once it is liquid add the oxtails in
   batches and brown.

3. Set the oxtails to one side and lower the heat. Now add the onions and
   fry until translucent.

4. Add the ginger and garlic and fry for 1 minute then add the oxtails and
   all the remaining ingredients except for the kidney beans. Stir well and
   bring to a gentle simmer, leave the mixture to cook for 2 hours stirring
   occasionally. Then add the kidney beans and cook for a further 10 minutes.

5. Serve with boiled rice and garlic bread.

Cottage Pie

Serves 4

Preparation:
10 mins

Cooking Time
45 mins
Approx

This is a handy way to use up leftover roast beef to make a tasty mid-week supper.

Ingredients

1 large onion, sliced

50g unsalted butter

500g of diced leftover roast beef

240ml beef gravy

4 diced cooked carrots

150g garden peas, cooked

Salt and pepper

500g mashed potato

2 tsp English mustard

1 bay leaf

How to cook

1. Preheat your oven to 200°C / 400°F / Gas mark 6 then melt half the butter in a frying pan and add the onions. Cook on a gentle heat until translucent.

2. Add the diced beef, gravy, carrots, peas, mustard and bay leaf. Heat through, season with salt and pepper, to taste.

3. Transfer to a baking dish, spoon the potatoes over the cottage pie mix.

4. Bake the pie for 30 minutes and serve with seasonal vegetables and extra gravy if desired.

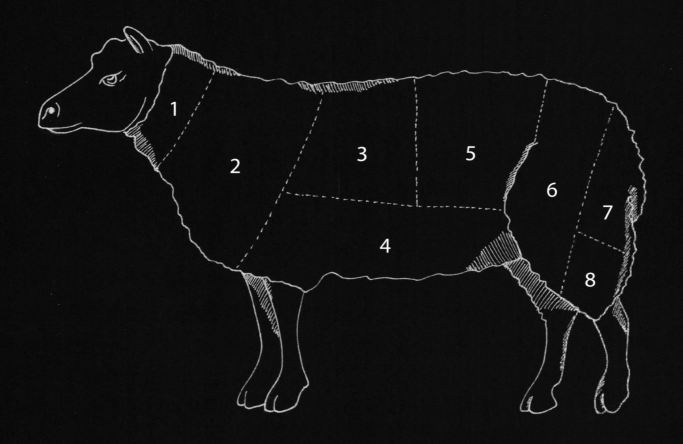

Lamb Cuts

1. Neck   4. Breast   7. Leg
2. Shoulder   5. Loin   8. Shank
3. Rack   6. Chump

Lamb
Recipes

The sight of lambs in lush green fields is a classic image of the British countryside which would not exist were it not for the hard work of responsible farmers. Your local butcher is the best place to buy traceable lamb as they can tell you about where it was produced and the quality of life it had.

Whilst young spring lamb is often the most talked about, lambs are usually at their prime in around mid-summer when the animals have had time to forage in the fields and develop their soft flavour.

Many people think that the ultimate lamb dish is a roasted leg with mint sauce. Whilst it is a tasty option, our leg of lamb with lavender and white wine recipe gives this classic dish an interesting twist.

If you prefer more comforting dishes you'll find our simple lamb hot pot recipe is a real winner. Should you prefer to be a bit more experimental the Persian lamb recipe uses rhubarb which adds a sharp edge to the sweet meat.

Whichever recipe you try from this section we hope you enjoy it. If you want to know more about the various lamb cuts why not go and talk to your local butcher.

Lancashire Hotpot

Serves 6

Preparation:
15mins

Cooking Time
3 hours 45 mins
Approx

Nothing could be better on a rainy afternoon than tucking into this wholesome warming dish. Just make sure you have a very sharp knife or a mandolin handy so that you can cut the potatoes to an even thickness.

Ingredients

1kg lamb stewing meat

1 large onion, thinly sliced

1kg peeled waxy potatoes

50g salted butter, melted

150ml vegetable stock

Salt and pepper

How to cook

1. Preheat your oven to 200°C / 400° F / Gas mark 6, meanwhile peel your potatoes and slice them into approximately 2mm thick discs.

2. Put the lamb into the bottom of a medium sized casserole dish and season with salt and pepper.

3. In a large frying pan sweat the onions and 25g of the butter until they are translucent.

4. Once cooked pour the onions over the lamb and layer the potato discs on top of the lamb until they are all used up.

5. Pour the stock over the hotpot and dot the remaining butter over the top of the potatoes. Cover the dish with foil and place it in the oven for 30 minutes then reduce the heat to 130°C / 250° F / Gas mark ½ and cook for a further 2 ½ hours.

6. Remove the dish from the oven and pre-heat the grill to maximum. Remove the foil and grill the potatoes for roughly 5-10mins until golden.

7. Serve with your choice of vegetables.

Persian Lamb

Serves 6

Preparation:
10mins

Cooking Time
1 hour 45 mins

This dish has a really fresh feel to it and the rhubarb adds a nice tart edge to the sweetness of the lamb and herbs. Your local butcher can provide you with excellent lamb shoulder to make this tasty dish.

Ingredients

1 kilo boneless lamb shoulder, diced

400g rhubarb

2 tbsp vegetable oil

90g butter

1 large onion, diced

1 garlic clove, crushed

2 tsp ground coriander

800ml vegetable stock

Handful fresh parsley, roughly chopped

Handful fresh mint leaves, chopped, plus extra to garnish

How to cook

1. Heat the oil and 30g butter in a large pan over a medium heat, add the onions and cook for 5 minutes. Then add the garlic and cook for 1 minute. Set aside in a bowl.

2. Increase the heat, add the lamb in batches and brown. Return the onion mixture to the pan, add the coriander and cook for 1 minute. Add the stock, cover and simmer gently for 1 hour.

3. Heat 30g butter in a small pan over a medium heat then add the herbs and cook for 8 minutes. Stir the herb mixture into the stew and simmer, half-covered, for 30 minutes, until the lamb is really tender.

4. Meanwhile, cut the rhubarb into 2.5cm lengths. Melt the remaining 30g butter in a large frying pan over a medium-high heat. Add the rhubarb, and cook, stirring, for 3-4 minutes, until just tender.

5. Stir the rhubarb into the stew and cook for 5 minutes. Pour into a large serving dish and scatter with mint and serve with couscous or rice.

Crown of English Spring Lamb

Serves 4

Preparation:
10 mins

Cooking Time
1 hour
Approx

This dish has the real wow factor when you bring it to the table making it great for dinner parties or special family meals. Your local butcher can French trim the lamb and shape it into a crown for you (this really isn't something you should try at home).

Ingredients

2 x racks of lamb (best end),
French trimmed

For the stuffing:

3 tbsp olive oil

1 onion, finely chopped

6 slices of white bread

½ tsp ground cinnamon

2 eating apples, peeled,
cored and chopped

1 orange, zest only

1 lemon, zest only

Bunch fresh parsley, chopped

1 tbsp chopped fresh thyme

Sea salt and freshly ground
black pepper

How to cook

1. Preheat the oven to 200° C / 400° F / Gas mark 6.

2. For the stuffing, heat the oil in a large frying pan. Add the onion and fry gently for five minutes, stirring occasionally until softened. Put the bread slices into a food processor and pulse them until they become fine breadcrumbs.

3. Sprinkle the cinnamon over the onion and cook for one minute. Scatter the apple pieces into the pan and add the orange and lemon zest. Stir together over a medium heat for 1-2 minutes. Add all the herbs and season with salt and freshly ground black pepper. Cook for a further minute, remove from the heat and set aside to cool.

4. Season the racks of lamb with salt and freshly ground black pepper. Place the racks onto a large, sturdy roasting tin with the eye of the meat at the bottom.

5. Spoon the stuffing into the centre of the ribs and cover the surface with roasting foil. Cover the ends of all the bones with foil to avoid burning.

6. Roast the crown for 45 minutes for pink and an extra 15 minutes if you prefer your lamb medium. Remove the foil five minutes before the end of the cooking time.

7. Remove the baking tin from the oven and carefully transfer the lamb and stuffing to a serving platter. Cover with foil and a tea towel. Set aside for 10-15 minutes.

8. Take the lamb to the table and cut through the bones to serve. Depending on the size of your racks, 2-3 chops should make one serving when accompanied by the fruity stuffing.

Cherry Glazed Lamb Chops

Serves 4

Preparation:
10mins

Cooking Time
20mins
Approx

These tasty chops are quick and easy to prepare but still looks stunning on the plate.

Ingredients

1 tsp chopped fresh rosemary

8 lamb loin chops trimmed
    by your butcher

2 tsp garlic puree

200ml vegetable stock

25g morello cherry jam

2 tbsp balsamic vinegar

Vegetable oil

Salt and pepper

How to cook

1. Put the rosemary and a pinch of salt and pepper in a bowl, and then
   rub the mixture onto the lamb.

2. Heat a little oil in a heavy-bottomed frying pan, add the lamb
   (in batches depending on the size) and cook for 5 minutes on
   each side. Remove the meat from the pan and set to one side.

3. Add a little more oil, garlic and stock and cook for 1 minute.
   Now stir in the jam and vinegar. Cook for a few minutes so that
   the sauce becomes nice and thick.

4. Return the lamb to the pan and cover liberally in the sauce.
   Serve with the vegetables of your choice.

Lamb Cutlets in Pastry

Serves 4

Preparation:
10 mins

Cooking Time
35 mins
Approx

These cutlets are a twist on traditional grilled cutlets the crunchy pastry layer gives way to soft delicious lamb.

Ingredients

8 lamb cutlets

175g any good liver pâté

1 packet of chilled short crust pastry
(you may need more depending on
the size of the cutlets)

1 egg, beaten

How to cook

1. Preheat a medium grill.

2. Grill the cutlets for 5 minutes turning half-way through, drain off any fat and set the cutlets to one side.

3. Preheat the oven to 200°C / 400° F / Gas mark 6.

4. Spread equal amounts of pâté over the chops then roll out the pastry. Cut the pastry into squares and wrap around each of the cutlets.

5. Lay the cutlets on a baking tray covered with a layer of greaseproof paper and brush a little beaten egg over each cutlet.

6. Cook for 30 minutes and serve immediately with vegetables of your choice.

Lamb Chump Chops with Herb Butter

Serves 6

Preparation: 15mins

Cooking Time 15mins Approx

Marinating these chops before grilling makes them that bit more mouth-watering.

Ingredients

6 lamb chump chops

For the marinade:

3 tbsp olive oil

2 tbsp dry cider

1 clove of garlic, finely sliced

Salt and pepper

For the herb butter:

50g butter

½ tsp malt vinegar

1 tsp freshly chopped mint

Salt and pepper

How to cook

1. Prepare the butter the day before you make this dish. Cream the butter until soft and gradually work in the vinegar. Beat in the freshly chopped mint and season with salt and pepper to taste.

2. Spoon the butter into a large square of greaseproof paper and roll it up into a log shape taking care to ensure the ends are sealed well like a cracker. Place in the fridge to chill overnight.

3. Preheat your grill to its maximum setting then mix all the marinade ingredients together in a shallow dish. Place all the chops in the dish and leave them to marinate for about 10 minutes, turning the meat half way through this time to ensure an even coating.

4. Lift the chops from the marinade and arrange on the grill pan and place roughly 10 cm below the grill for 15 minutes turning halfway through the cooking time.

5. When the chops are cooked remove from the heat and place a slice of the butter on top of each chop. Serve with a selection of vegetables.

LAMB

Roast Loin of Lamb with Herbs

Serves 6

Preparation: 10mins

Cooking Time 2 hours Approx

Lamb has a lovely sweet quality to it, serving it with this variety of herbs complement it perfectly.

Ingredients

1.75 kilo loin of lamb, boned but not rolled with the fat left on

Salt and pepper

Small bunch of fresh mint, finely chopped

Small bunch of flat leaf parsley, finely chopped

1 tbsp fresh rosemary, finely chopped

Pinch of sugar

A little butcher's string

How to cook

1. Preheat your oven to 180°C / 350°F / Gas mark 4

2. Open the meat out, lay it fat side down and sprinkle with salt and pepper. Put all the herbs and sugar into a pestle and mortar (or use a mixing bowl with a rolling pin) and gently pound the leaves until they are slightly bruised.

3. Spread the herb mixture evenly across the lamb then roll up the meat from the thicker side and secure with the string.

4. Roast in the centre of the oven for 1 ¾ hours. If you would like your lamb to be well done cook for 2 hours. Remove the lamb from the oven and serve with vegetables of your choice.

Lamb Noisette

Serves 6

Preparation: 10 mins

Cooking Time 1 ½ hours Approx

This dish is a real one pot wonder that takes minutes to prepare so once it's in the oven all you have to think about is how you are going to serve it. Your butcher can prepare the Noisettes for you.

Ingredients

6 Lamb Noisettes

1 tbsp flour, seasoned with salt & pepper

25g butter

1 large white onion, finely sliced

Pinch of dried rosemary

1 tbsp finely chopped parsley

300ml red wine

100g button mushrooms

12 new potatoes, cut in half

1 packet of frozen peas

2 minced cloves of garlic

Butchers' string

How to cook

1. Preheat your oven to 180°C / 350°F / Gas mark 4.

2. Dust the lamb with the flour and heat the butter in a large frying pan, fry the meat in the pan for about 15-20mins to ensure that all the sides of the meat are sealed.

3. Remove the lamb from the pan and place it in a large casserole dish, add the onion to the frying pan and fry gently until the onions are starting to brown slightly. Add the onion to the casserole dish along with the rosemary.

4. Pour away some of the frying pan liquor until there is about 1 tbsp of liquid left, then add garlic and fry on a low heat for 1 minute. Next add the wine and bring it to the boil to cook off the alcohol.

5. Add the wine to the casserole dish along with the mushrooms, potatoes and parsley. Cover the whole dish with a lid of grease proof paper that has been buttered on the underside. Secure it with butcher's string (your butcher can provide you with this).

6. Cook in the centre of the oven for 1 hour then add the peas to the dish and cook for a further 10 minutes. Remove the string from the lamb and serve.

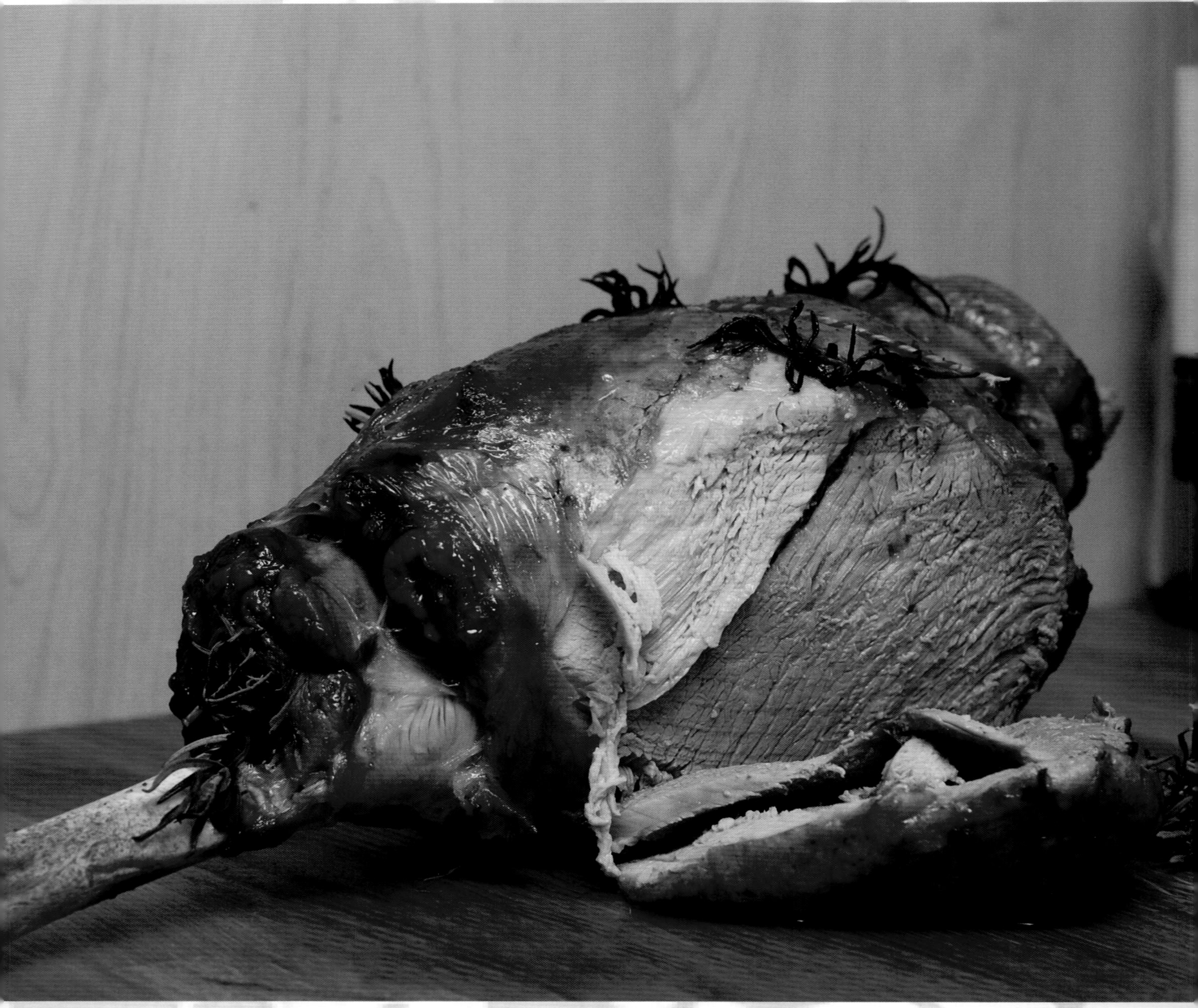

Leg of Lamb with Wine and Lavender

Serves   4-6

Preparation:
5 mins

Cooking Time
3 ½ hours
Approx

This is a creative twist on the traditional roast leg of lamb.

Ingredients

2 kg leg of lamb bone in

1 bottle dry white wine

A few sprigs of fresh lavender

Salt and black pepper

How to cook

1. Preheat the oven to 170°C / 325°F / Gas 3.

2. Season the lamb with salt and pepper and place in a large roasting dish on a medium hob. Turn the leg continuously for 5-10 minutes to ensure the meat is well sealed.

3. Remove from the heat and using a sharp knife make several holes in the leg of lamb to place the lavender sprigs into the meat.

4. Add the wine to the pan and place it back onto the hob, and bring to the boil then transfer the dish to the oven for 3-3 ½ hours.

5. Baste the meat at regular intervals and if you think it might be drying out cover it with foil or add more wine as you see fit.

6. Remove the lamb from the oven and allow it to rest. Meanwhile return the pan to the hob and reduce the cooking liquor to make a tasty gravy, this should take about 10-15 minutes depending on how much liquid there is.

7. Serve with the gravy and your choice of vegetables.

Lamb Shank

Serves 2

Preparation:
10mins

Cooking Time
3 hours
Approx

This slow cooked dish is perfect for dinner parties and looks stunning on the plate. Your butcher can help you to choose the best sized shanks depending on the size of your guests' appetite.

Ingredients

2 lamb shanks

50g bacon lardons

1 chopped carrot

1 large white onion, sliced

2 tsp tomato puree

½ wine glass Marsala wine

½ wine glass of port

1 tsp paprika

1 tsp ginger powder

125ml beef stock

1 tsp peppercorns

1 star anise

2 tsp apricot jam

1 bulb of garlic, halved

2 bay leaves

Salt and pepper

Vegetable oil

How to cook

1. Preheat your oven to 180°C / 350° F / Gas mark 4. In a bowl season the shanks with salt and pepper.

2. Heat a little oil in a large oven proof casserole pot that can be used on the hob and brown off the shanks and set to one side. Now add the lardons and fry for 2 minutes.

3. Add the carrots and onion and allow to soften for 5 minutes, then add the tomato puree and cook for 1 minute.

4. Add the Masala wine and port and leave to cook for one minute to cook off the alcohol.

5. Now add the beef stock, star anise, garlic, bay leaves, pepper corns, paprika, ginger and apricot jam and stir well.

6. Add the shanks ensuring the liquid covers the shanks, if it doesn't just add some water.

7. Cover and place in the oven for 3 hours turning the shanks regularly.

8. When they are done remove them from the dish, put onto warmed plates and remove the garlic bulbs, pepper corns and star anise from the sauce. Pour the sauce over the shanks and serve.

Lamb Rogan Josh

Serves 4

Preparation:
10mins

Cooking Time
1 hour 15 mins
Approx

Lamb neck is a hard working cut of meat that adds a rich flavour to this dish. Once you have made this curry you won't want to call the takeaway again. You will need a food processor to create the Rogan Josh paste.

Ingredients

1 large onion, sliced

4 cloves of garlic

5cm sized piece of ginger, diced

1 tsp ground cinnamon

2 tsp ground cumin

1 tbsp hot paprika

1 tsp chilli powder

1 tsp salt

1 tbsp tomato puree

2 tbsp vegetable oil

1 kilo lamb neck cut, diced

8 coriander seeds, lightly crushed

300 ml vegetable stock

How to cook

1. Using a food processor blend together the garlic, onion, ginger, tomato puree and all of the ground spices until it forms a paste.

2. Heat a small amount of oil in a large pan and add the lamb and coriander seeds, cook until the lamb is brown all over.

3. Stir in the spice paste and cook for 5 minutes. Pour in the stock and bring to a simmer. Pop on the lid and cook for 1 hour stirring occasionally until the sauce has thickened.

4. Serve with rice and naan breads.

Devilled Lamb Kidneys

Serves 2

Preparation:
10mins

Cooking Time
20mins
Approx

This dish makes a great starter or quick and tasty lunchtime snack. Kidneys are really underrated and this recipe shows them off at their best. Ask your butcher to de-core the kidneys and slice them in half to take the hard work out of this recipe for you.

Ingredients

4 lamb kidneys
(de-cored and cut in half)

2 tbsp flour

2 small shallots, finely sliced

1 clove garlic, finely sliced

1 tbsp cayenne pepper

2 tbsp English mustard powder

A few drops of Worcestershire sauce

A few drops of Tabasco

100ml vegetable stock

2 tbsp double cream

2 tbsp chopped parsley

25g butter

How to cook

1. Take a large heavy bottomed frying pan and bring it up to a high heat.

2. In a large bowl mix the flour, cayenne pepper and mustard powder together.

3. Toss the kidneys in the flour until they are thoroughly coated.

4. Add the butter to the pan. When melted add the kidneys and cook for 1 minute on either side.

5. Remove kidneys from the pan and leave to rest.

6. In the same pan add the shallots and garlic and fry for 2 minutes. Add the Worchestershire sauce and Tabasco.

7. Stir well and add the stock and reduce by half.

8. Add cream then boil. Add kidneys to reheat for 30 seconds then add parsley.

9. Serve straight away. It is lovely on hot buttered toast.

Lamb's Kidney with Lentils

Serves 4

Preparation:
5 mins

Cooking Time
20 mins
Approx

This dish isn't just cost effective, it's a wholesome and tasty way to enjoy kidneys. Ask your butcher to de-core and half the kidneys for you.

Ingredients

500g lamb's kidneys

2 tbsp olive oil

2 cloves garlic, finely chopped

1 tsp chill powder

1 glass of red wine

150ml double cream

150g green lentils, cooked
and drained

1 tbsp finely chopped parsley

Salt and freshly ground black pepper

How to cook

1. Heat the oil in a large, heavy frying pan over a high heat. Add the garlic and a few seconds later, the kidneys. Fry for barely a minute, tossing them in the pan, until they are nicely browned.

2. Add the chilli powder and pour in the wine. Cook until the liquor has reduced by half.

3. Add the cream, a good pinch of salt and a few twists of pepper, and boil to reduce still further.

4. When the sauce is glossy and nicely coating the kidneys (not much more than 7 or 8 minutes after the kidneys first went in), add the lentils, mix well and heat through for just 1 minute.

5. Serve at once sprinkled with the parsley.

Lamb's Liver Pâté with Spicy Pepper Salad

 Serves 4

 Preparation: 15mins

 Cooking Time 15 mins Approx

The zingy pepper salad contrasts well with the creamy texture of the pâté, it makes a great starter or can be served as a snack at parties. This dish requires overnight refrigeration for the salad.

Ingredients

For the pepper salad:

1 jar of grilled peppers, finely sliced

1 red onion, finely sliced

4 tbsp olive oil

4 tbsp balsamic vinegar

Salt and pepper

A few shakes of Tabasco (optional)

For the pâté:

450g lamb's liver, cut into thin strips by your butcher

1 red onion, finely sliced

2 cloves of garlic, finely chopped

250g unsalted butter, cubed

Salt and pepper

How to cook

1. In a bowl mix the peppers, onion, oil and balsamic vinegar, then add the salt, pepper and Tabasco (optional) to suit your pallet. Cover with cling film and store in the fridge overnight.

2. Gently soften the onions with about a quarter of the butter in a pan.

3. Now add the liver to the pan and half the butter and cook for around 7 minutes. Add the garlic to the pan about 1 minute before the end of cooking.

4. Stir well and add the remaining butter. Cook until the liver is done, this will take a few minutes. You can test by cutting a piece; it should be slightly grey throughout.

5. Once the liver is cooked remove it from the pan. Don't throw away the buttery liquid you'll need that for later.

6. Put the onions and liver into a food processor and blend until it becomes a smooth paste. Add salt and pepper to taste.

7. Pour the mixture into either four ramekins or one large dish, depending on how you want to present the pate. Pour the reserved buttery liquid over the top and cover with cling film. Leave overnight in the fridge to set.

8. Serve with crusty bread topped with the pepper salad.

Lamb's Liver Stroganoff

Serves 4

Preparation: 10mins

Cooking Time 15mins

This is a great and different way to enjoy lamb's liver as opposed to the usual liver and onions.

Ingredients

450g lamb's liver

1 large onion, finely sliced

250g of mushrooms, sliced

400ml carton crème fraîche

150ml dry white wine

2 tsp olive oil

50g of salted butter

1 tsp wholegrain mustard

Salt and freshly ground black pepper

Small bunch of fresh flat leaf parsley

How to cook

1. Using a sharp knife, slice the liver into thin small strips.

2. Now add the olive oil to a large frying-pan or sauté pan over a high heat, add the onion, then turn the heat down to medium and cook for 5 minutes while stirring.

3. After that add half of the butter, when melted add the sliced mushrooms and cook these for a further 5 minutes.

4. Now transfer the onions and mushrooms to a warm plate with a slotted spoon leaving all the juices in the pan and cover with foil.

5. Add the remaining butter to the pan over a high heat then add the strips of liver and cook for only about one or two minutes while tossing them.

6. Add the wine and bring to a boil then simmer for 1 minute before returning the onions and mushrooms to the pan.

7. Now season to your taste, add the crème fraîche and mustard and gently stir to combine everything evenly. Add the parsley.

8. Serve on a warm plate with boiled rice.

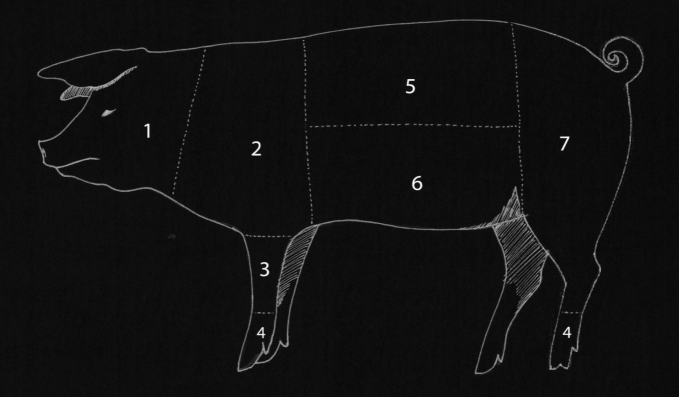

Pork Cuts

1. Head   4. Trotter   6. Belly
2. Shoulder   5. Loin   7. Leg
3. Hock

Pork
Recipes

Your local butcher will be able to show you that there is more to pork than bacon sandwiches and chops. A good butcher will work closely with farmers to ensure that the pork they are selling has been raised in good conditions so that you receive a top quality product.

If you love crispy cracking why not try our pork belly recipe or if it is sausages you love why not try the toad in the hole or the sausage casserole recipe? British butchers' sausages are far superior in quality to anything you can buy from a supermarket this is because of the care and attention they put into making each one. Many butchers guard their sausage mix recipes with great secrecy, only passing it when they hand the business over to the next generation.

Whatever you choose to cook from this chapter, make sure you visit your local butcher for the finest quality pork.

Pork Chops with a Mustard and Cider Sauce

Serves 4

Preparation: 10 mins

Cooking Time 45 mins

Supermarket bought chops simply will not work in this recipe - when meat is stored in plastic packets it sweats and this makes for a watery sauce. Butcher bought chops are always best and have a better covering of fat which in term gives the dish flavour.

Ingredients

4 pork chops

25g unsalted butter

1 onion, thinly sliced

25g plain flour

150ml dry cider

75ml good vegetable stock

1 garlic clove, thinly sliced

2 tbsp double cream

2 heaped tsp wholegrain mustard

Salt and pepper

How to cook

1. Preheat your oven to 190°C / 375° F / Gas mark 5 then fry the pork chops in a large pan with the butter and onions until the chops are brown on both sides.

2. Remove the chops and continue cooking the onions until they are soft. Add the garlic and then the flour to the pan and cook for 2 minutes.

3. Stir in the cider and stock stirring constantly to ensure that no lumps form. Add the cream, mustard and salt and pepper to taste.

4. Place the chops into a shallow baking tray lined with baking foil and pour the sauce over the top of them.

5. Bake the chops in the oven for 30 – 40 minutes. Serve with seasonal vegetables.

Crispy Pork Belly

Serves 6

Preparation:
10 mins

Cooking Time
3 hours
Approx

Nothing is more mouth watering than seeing perfect pork crackling, make sure you buy
your pork from your local butcher (ask them to leave th bone on). When the larger retailers
pack pork belly into plastic trays it sweats and stops the fat from crackling as well.

Ingredients

1 kilo piece of belly pork

1 bunch of fresh thyme,
  roughly chopped

2 tbsp flaked sea salt

1 tbsp olive oil

Juice of 1 lemon

How to cook

1. Preheat your oven to 200°C / 400° F / Gas mark 6

2. In a pestle and mortar (or a rolling pin in a mixing bowl) pound the
   salt, oil, thyme and lemon juice for about 1 minute until all the ingredients
   are combined.

3. Put the pork into a roasting tray and spread the mixture from the pestle
   and mortar across the fat ensuring that it goes into the cuts too.

4. Place the pork in the centre of the oven and cook for 30 minutes then turn
   the heat down to 180°C / 350° F/ Gas 4 and roast for a further 2 hrs.

5. Finally, turn the heat back up to 220°C / 425° F/ Gas 7 for around 30 minutes
   or until the crackling is really crispy.

6. Remove the pork from the oven and cover with foil for 20 minutes. Serve
   with apple sauce and vegetables of your choice.

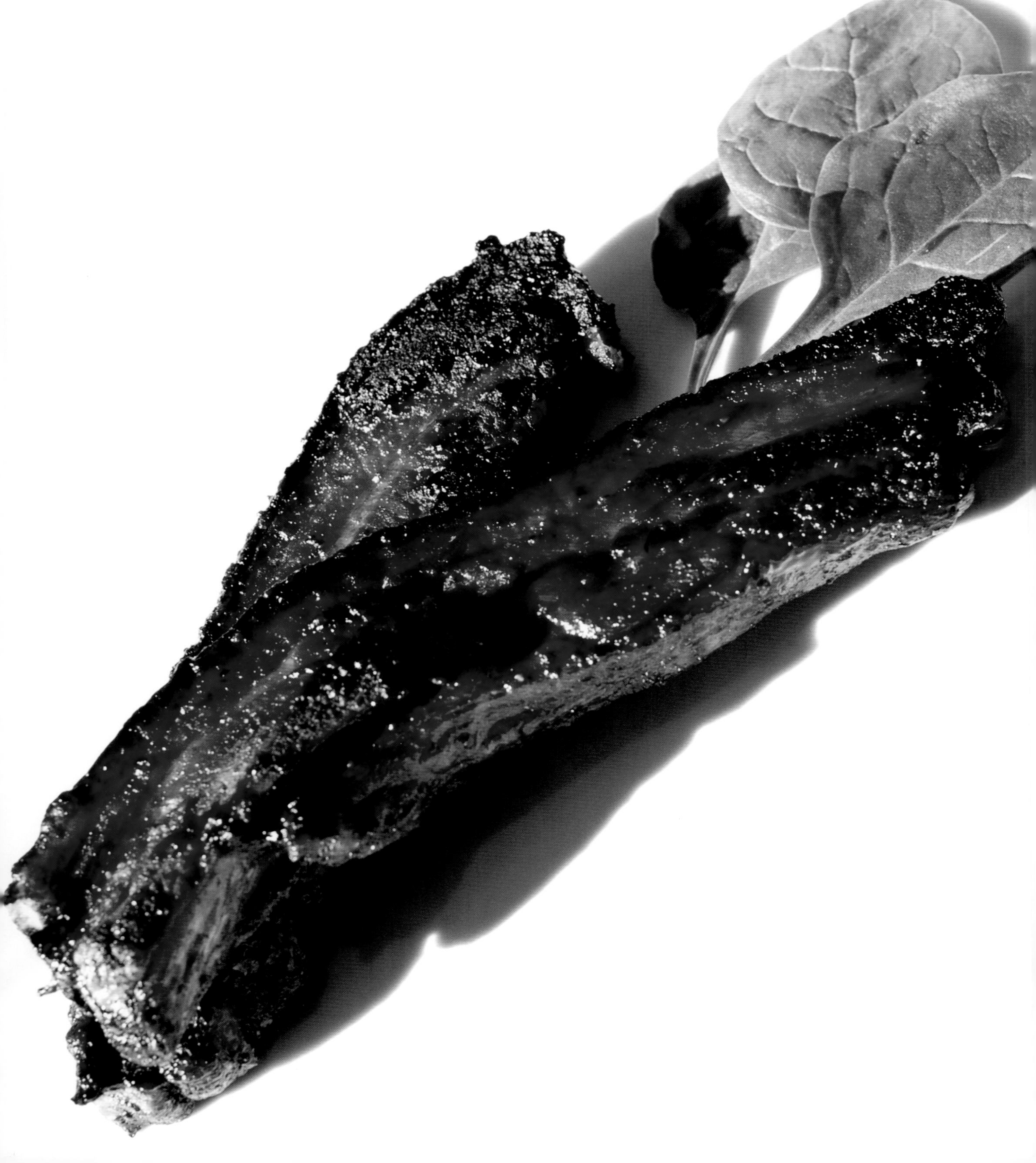

Pork Belly Strips with Barbecue Sauce

Serves 2

Preparation: 10mins

Cooking Time 40 mins Approx

Pork belly is a really tasty forgotten cut, it is always best bought from your local butcher as supermarket pork is wrapped in plastic which makes the meat sweat and prevents it from crisping up.

Ingredients

4 pork belly strips

2 tbsp light olive oil

5 tbsp dry cider

5 tbsp dark soy sauce

1 tbsp tomato puree

1 heaped tsp of ground ginger

2 garlic cloves, peeled and crushed

2 tbsp light brown sugar

2 tsp mustard powder

1 tbsp cider vinegar

Salt and pepper

How to cook

1. Preheat your oven to 200°C / 400°F / Gas mark 6. Salt and pepper both sides of the pork belly strips and place on a lightly oiled baking tray in the oven for 30 minutes.

2. Combine all the remaining ingredients in a bowl and mix together and set to one side.

3. Remove the pork after 30 minutes and cover both sides with the sauce.

4. If you are going to finish the strips on the barbeque put them back in the oven for another 10 minutes and then transfer them on to the barbeque and cook until golden. Otherwise return the strips to the oven and cook until golden, turn them regularly to ensure an even coating of sauce.

Cola Baked Ham

Serves 4

Preparation: 5mins

Cooking Time 2 hours 45 mins Approx

This is fantastic hot with salad and pickles or served cold sliced in sandwiches.

Ingredients

2kg boneless gammon joint

1 large white onion

15 whole cloves

2 litres cola

2 tbsp English mustard

2 tbsp dark brown sugar

How to cook

1. Some gammons need to be soaked overnight, just ask your butcher when buying your joint and they will be able to advise how to prepare your joint for cooking. If you do soak yours, make sure that you throw away all the salty water before commencing cooking.

2. Put your gammon into a large pot and cover with cola, a large 2 litre bottle should cover your gammon but top it up with water if you cannot completely cover the meat.

3. Peel the brown layers away from the onion and push 5 of the cloves into the white flesh. Add this to the pan and put the lid on.

4. Bring the liquid slowly to the boil and then reduce to a simmer, leave the pan on the heat for 2 ½ hours.

5. Remove the gammon from the pan and thoroughly pat dry with kitchen paper. Throw away the onion and cooking liquor. Place the gammon on a baking tray covered with foil.

6. Pre-heat the oven to 240° C / 425° F / Gas mark 9 and remove the top layer of fat from the gammon and score the remaining fat to create a crisscross pattern. Place the remaining cloves into intersections of the fat.

7. Mix together the mustard and sugar and cover the fat with the mixture. Now place the gammon in the oven for approximately 10 minutes or until the fat becomes golden and sticky.

8. Let the meat rest for at least 15 minutes after you bring it out of the oven before slicing.

Chilli Ham and Noodle Salad

Serves 4

Preparation:
5 mins

Cooking Time
10 mins
Approx

To make your cola baked ham go further why not try this recipe - it's quick simple making it a perfect mid-week meal.

Ingredients

500g cola baked ham, cut into bite size pieces

1 whole red chilli, finely chopped (optional)

2 nests of egg noodles

1 bunch spring onions

1 tbsp sweet chilli sauce

1 tsp fish sauce

1 tsp light soy sauce

Juice of one lime

Sesame oil

How to cook

1. Cook the noodles as per the instructions on the packet. Meanwhile combine the sweet chilli sauce, fish sauce, soy sauce and lime juice in a bowl.

2. Add the ham and finely slice the spring onions, toss well to coat everything in the sauce.

3. Drain the noodles well and add to the bowl. Drizzle a small amount of sesame oil into the bowl and toss all ingredients together to ensure they are combined well.

4. Sprinkle a little of the raw chilli on top if you would like some extra heat. Serve with prawn crackers and sweet chilli sauce.

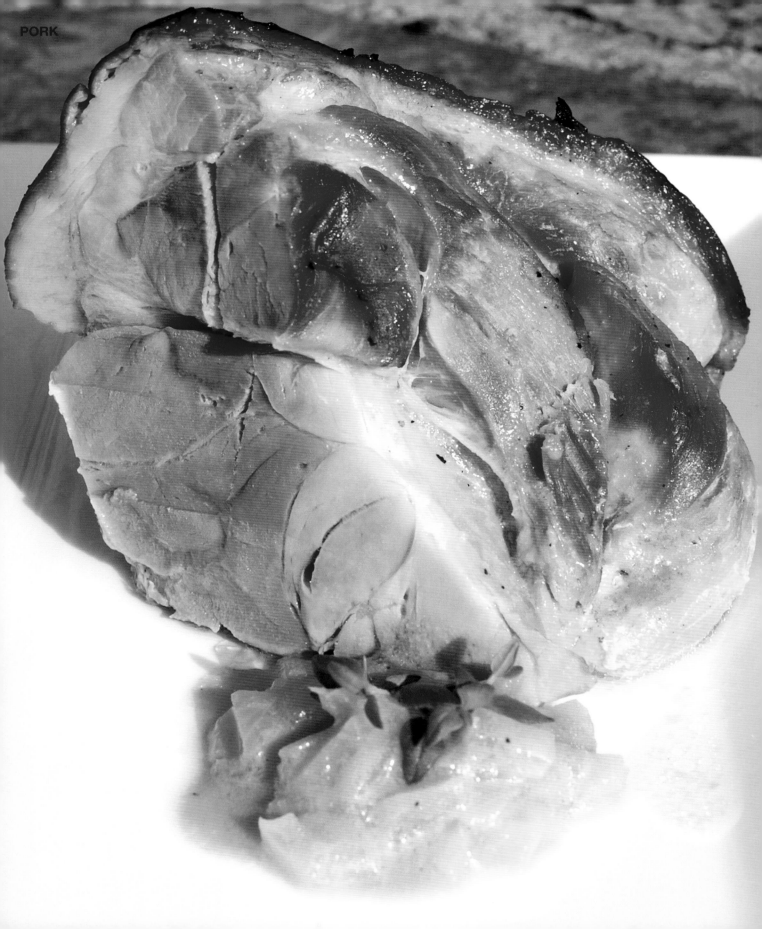

PORK

Ham Hock with Cider

Serves 6

Preparation:
15 mins

Cooking Time
2 ½ hours
Approx

A delicious recipe for all seasons using a cheap cut of pork, any leftovers can be used for sandwiches.

Ingredients

2 ham hocks (1.5kg each)

1 litre dry cider

4 small onions, halved, skin removed

1 tbsp black peppercorns

8 cloves

1 tbsp Demerara sugar

How to cook

1. Soak the hocks in a large pan of cold water overnight. Drain away the liquid and refil the pan with fresh water then transfer the pan to the hob and bring to the boil.

2. Drain and rinse the hocks, then put them into a pan with the cider, peppercorns, Demerara sugar and onions (stud these with the cloves). Top up the pan with water if the cider doesn't cover the hocks. Bring the pan to the boil then reduce to a simmer and cover. Cook the hocks for about 2 hours.

3. Take the hocks out of the stock and let them cool a little on a carving board before you slice it.

Pea and Ham Soup

Serves 2-4

Preparation:
5 mins

Cooking Time
30 mins
Approx

This is another way of using up any leftover ham you might have in the fridge. Perfect for warming you up on a cold winter's evening.

Ingredients

1 packet (quick soak) dried peas

1 white onion, finely chopped

600ml vegetable stock

Salt and pepper

As much leftover ham as you like

How to cook

1. Soak the peas according to the packet instructions.

2. Once the peas are soaked, transfer them to a colander in the sink and rinse well with cold water.

3. In a large pan combine the peas and stock, season with salt and pepper and bring to the boil.

4. Reduce the heat to a simmer and cook for 20-25 minutes. To finish, shred the ham into each bowl and ladle the soup on top. Serve with crusty bread.

Roast Pork Leg with Garlic & Thyme

Serves 8

Preparation: 5 mins

Cooking Time 3 hours

This recipe makes a tasty Sunday lunch and plenty of crispy crackling for all the family to enjoy, it's just as nice when sliced and served in sandwiches with apple sauce.

Ingredients

3kg pork leg - ask your butcher to score the fat

3 cloves of garlic, sliced

3 fresh bay leaves, chopped

100ml cider vinegar

1 tbsp dried thyme

Salt and pepper

How to cook

1. Preheat the oven to 180°C / 350° F / Gas mark 4. Place the pork fat side up into a roasting tray. Put the garlic into the scored fat and sprinkle salt and pepper over the pork.

2. Mix the vinegar, bay leaves and thyme in a bowl and pour over the pork.

3. Put the pork into the oven for 3 hours, basting frequently. Let the meat rest for 20 minutes under roasting foil before slicing.

Toad in the Hole

Serves 4

Preparation: 15 mins

Cooking Time 40 mins Approx

This is a classic dish that is best cooked with top quality butchers' sausage, if you use mass produced ones they tend to be watery which means that the batter doesn't crisp up well.

Ingredients

15g beef dripping

450g sausages

For the batter:

100g plain flour

¼ tsp salt

1 egg

300ml milk

How to cook

1. Preheat your oven to 200°C / 400°F / Gas mark 6

2. To prepare the batter sieve the flour and salt into a large mixing bowl and hollow out the centre of the flour.

3. Crack the egg into the well and one third of the milk and stir well. Add the remaining milk gradually stirring continuously. Transfer to a jug and leave to stand.

4. Place the sausages and dripping in a roasting tin and place in the top of the oven until the fat becomes very hot. This should take no longer than 10 minutes.

5. Pour the batter into the roasting tin and leave to cook in the oven for 25-30 minutes. The batter should be well risen and crispy.

6. Serve with lots of gravy and mashed potatoes.

Sausage Casserole

Serves 6

Preperation:
5 mins

Cooking Time
40 mins
Approx

If you only have sausages as part of a full-English then this recipe is for you! It's a great family meal, just be sure to use top quality butchers' sausages. Mass produced sausages make the sauce rather watery and unappealing.

Ingredients

12 butchers' pork sausages

1 large onion, sliced

2 garlic cloves, crushed

1 tsp powdered cumin

1 can tinned tomatoes

300ml vegetable stock

2 tbsp tomato puree

1 tbsp Worcestershire sauce

1 tbsp barbeque sauce

1 tsp cayenne pepper

2 bay leaves

100ml dry cider

1 can red kidney beans

Sunflower oil

Salt and pepper

How to cook

1. Preheat the oven to 200°C / 400° F / Gas mark 6 and put all the ingredients except for the kidney beans into a large casserole dish, mix well. Put in the oven for 30 minutes stirring occasionally.

2. Wash the beans under cold running water, drain and stir into the casserole. Cook in the oven for a further 10 minutes without the lid.

3. The sauce should be rich and thick, if not leave it in the oven for another few minutes. Serve with boiled rice or crusty bread.

Mock Goose Pie

 Serves 6

 Preparation: 15 mins

 Cooking Time 30 mins Approx

This dish is quick and simple to prepare using everyday ingredients and offers a creative alternative to sausages and mash.

Ingredients

500g sausage meat

500g cooked mashed potato

1 packet of ready-made stuffing mix

How to cook

1. Preheat your oven to 200°C / 400°F / Gas mark 6 and make the stuffing as per the packet instructions.

2. Spread the sausage meat across the bottom of the dish, then add an even layer of stuffing. Top the pie off with a layer of mash and use a fork to create a nice pattern.

3. Transfer the dish to the oven and bake the pie for 30 minutes, serve with gravy and vegetables of your choice.

Cheese and Bacon Scones

Serves 4-6

Preparation:
15 mins

Cooking Time
15 mins
Approx

These go down a treat and are a great tea time alternative to jam and scones. The trick here is to buy top notch bacon from your butcher. Mass produced bacon often leaves a lot of water in the pan and this results in soggy scones, and no one wants that.

Ingredients

3 rashers of bacon, finely chopped

200g self-raising flour

1 tsp mustard powder

1 pinch cayenne pepper
or more if you like heat

40g salted butter, cubed

100g grated mature Cheddar cheese

100ml semi-skimmed milk

How to cook

1. Preheat the oven to 200°C / 400° F / Gas mark 6 and lightly grease a baking tray.

2. Cook the bacon in a dry pan over a low heat until slightly brown but not too crispy.

3. In a bowl or blender mix the flour, mustard powder and cayenne pepper, then rub in the butter until the mixture resembles fine breadcrumbs.

4. Add the cheese and bacon to the flour mixture, and then gradually stir in the milk until the mixture binds and becomes dough like.

5. Lightly flour your work surface and roll out the dough and cut into discs using a 5cm wide cutter. The scones should be about 2cm thick. Re-roll the dough and cut until it has all been used.

6. Place your scones onto the baking sheet and brush with a little milk on top. Transfer them to the oven and allow them to bake for 10-15 minutes.

7. Remove from the oven and try to resist the urge to eat them straight away (if you can).

Pig Liver Pâté with a Sage Crust

Serves 4

Preparation: 5 mins

Cooking Time 2 mins Approx

Sage compliments the rich taste of liver well and this makes a great starter for four people. Your local butcher can take the hassle out of preparing the pig livers for you.

Ingredients

500g pig's liver sliced into 1cm strips

4 tbsp plain flour

1 small bunch fresh sage

1 tbsp vegetable oil

Salt and pepper

How to cook

1. Put the flour, sage and a little salt and pepper into a food processor and blend until the sage has been completely incorporated into the flour. Pour the mixture into a bowl and add the liver.

2. Ensure the liver slices are thoroughly coated in the flour mixture, pour a little oil into a large frying pan. Once it's very hot add the liver slices and cook for 30 seconds turning constantly.

3. Serve on slices of toasted buttered bread.

Accompaniments

Mint Sauce

There is nothing better than freshly made mint sauce to compliment roast lamb dishes. For a more hotter tasting sauce add some thinly sliced white onion. This sauce should keep for 2-3 months in cold storage or for 6-8 months in the refrigerator

Serves 4

Preparation: 10 mins

Cooking Time: 25 mins

Ingredients

4 tbsp fresh mint leaves, finely chopped

3 tbsp vinegar

1 tbsp caster sugar

3 tbsp boiling water

1 tsp salt

How to cook

1. Rinse mint leaves, strip from the stems, and chop into fine pieces. Alternatively process in a blender for about 10 seconds.

2. Bring the vinegar to a simmer in a small saucepan, then add the sugar and chopped leaves. Simmer for about 20 minutes to infuse. Add a little water to taste, depending on how strong or how sweet you want the sauce.

3. You can increase this recipe to make enough for future use. Sterilise some jam jars and fill with the sauce while the jars are still warm. Seal tightly.

Apple Sauce

This is a classic sauce to go with roast pork but we also like it with cold slices of pork in a sandwich.

Serves 6

Preparation: 10 mins

Cooking Time 15 mins

Ingredients

500g Bramley apples, peeled, cored and chopped

50g caster sugar

25g unsalted butter, cubed

How to cook

1. Put the chopped apples and sugar into a saucepan with 150ml of cold water and the sugar. Bring to simmering point then cover with the lid and leave for 10-15 minutes.

2. Remove the lid and stir well until all the liquid has evaporated then turn off the heat and stir in the butter.

Bubble and Squeak

This dish is a great way of using up leftovers from your Sunday roast. If you haven't made it before you will find it becomes a real family favourite.

 Serves 4

 Preparation: 10 mins

 Cooking Time: 20 mins

Ingredients

1 red onion, finely chopped

4 rashers streaky bacon, cut into small pieces

450g leftover mashed potato

300g leftover mixed cooked vegetables chopped into bite size pieces

Salt and pepper to taste

25g butter

2 tbsp plain flour

How to cook

1. Combine the mash and vegetables in a large mixing bowl.

2. On a low heat melt half the butter in a frying pan and cook the onion until translucent, add the bacon and cook until crispy.

3. Using a slotted spoon remove the onions and bacon from the pan and add to the mash mixture. Don't clean out the pan you want to keep the flavour from the bacon and butter.

4. Using your hands, take golf ball sized portions and cover them lightly with flour, melt the remaining butter in the pan.

5. Place the patties, no more than four at a time in the pan so you have room to flip them and fry until golden brown. Serve with slices of cold beef and pickles of your choice.

Sour Cream and Horseradish Sauce

This sauce is a classic accompaniment to roast beef. You can increase the strength of the sauce by adding more horseradish root.

Serves 6

Preparation:
10 mins

Ingredients

227g sour cream

20cm horseradish root

1 teaspoon coarsely ground pepper

1 tsp Worcestershire sauce

1 tbsp warm water

How to cook

1. Ensure that you are working in a well-ventilated room as fresh horseradish is more potent than chopped onions.

2. Peel and chop the horseradish into small chunks and place in a food process with the water. Pulse until the root becomes a paste.

3. Working quickly, transfer all the other sauce ingredients to the food processor and mix well.

Persian-Style Herb Rice

Serves 6

Preparation:
10mins plus
overnight
soaking

Cooking Time
1 hour

This recipe goes very well with the Persian lamb dish. It is an interesting twist and a change from the usual boiled or steamed rice dishes western cuisine usually favours.

Ingredients

500g basmati rice

1 bunch fresh coriander

1 bunch fresh parsley

1 bunch fresh chives

Vegetable oil

250g butter divided into 4 blocks

Sea salt crystals

How to cook

1. Place your rice in a large bowl and fill with cold water, drain the rice through a sieve and return to the bowl.

2. Repeat this process until the water runs clear, once this is done put the drained rice back in the bowl and cover with water and add a good handful of sea salt. Cover the bowl with cling film and leave overnight.

3. Put all the herbs into a food processor (you may need to do this in batches).

4. Fill a large cooking pot with two kettles worth of boiling water, drain the rice well and add to the pot with the herbs. Bring to the boil and cook for 10 minutes, then drain the rice and herbs in a sieve which you may need to do in batches. The sieve will retain the herbs better than a colander.

5. Return your cooking pot to the hob and add three table spoons of vegetable oil, two blocks of butter and a generous handful of sea salt crystals.

6. Scatter the rice into the pan to ensure it remains fluffy and add the two remaining blocks of butter.

7. Now wrap a tea towel around the cooking pot lid and place on top, cook on a medium heat for around 10 minutes. Then reduce the heat to the lowest setting and cook for a further 25 to 30 minutes.

8. Pour the rice into a large serving bowl and scrap the crispy rice out from the bottom of the pan and serve on top.